DRONES ARE EVERYWHERE!

DRONES
FOR PHOTOGRAPHY

CHRISTINE HONDERS

PowerKiDS press
New York

Published in 2020 by The Rosen Publishing Group, Inc.
29 East 21st Street, New York, NY 10010

First Edition

Editor: Shannon Harts
Book Design: Tanya Dellaccio

Photo Credits: Cover (background) Przemek Klos/Shutterstock.com; cover (drone) Kypros/Moment/Getty Images; series background Djem/Shuttertock.com; p. 5 Barcroft Media/Getty Images; p. 6 Dutourdumonde Photography/Shutterstock.com; p. 7 Pikovit/Shutterstock.com; p. 8 https://upload.wikimedia.org/wikipedia/commons/e/ee/Boeing_X-37B_inside_payload_fairing_before_launch.jpg; p. 9 Handout/Getty Images News/Getty Images; p. 11 (inset) Leonid Eremeychuk/Shutterstock.com; p. 11 (main) JOE KLAMAR/AFP/Getty Images; p. 13 Richard Whitcombe/Shutterstock.com; p. 15 Anadolu Agency/Getty Images; p. 17 MediaNews Group/The Mercury News via Getty Images/Getty Images; p. 19 Artyom Korotayev/TASS/Getty Images; p. 21 Den Rozhnovsky/Shutterstock.com; p. 22 Dmitry Kalinovsky/Shutterstock.com.

Cataloging-in-Publication Data

Names: Honders, Christine.
Title: Drones for photography / Christine Honders.
Description: New York : PowerKids Press, 2020. | Series: Drones are everywhere! | Includes glossary and index.
Identifiers: ISBN 9781725309265 (pbk.) | ISBN 9781725309289 (library bound) | ISBN 9781725309272 (6 pack)
Subjects: LCSH: Drone aircraft–Juvenile literature. | Aerial photography–Juvenile literature.
Classification: LCC UG1242.D7 H5866 2020 | DDC 623.74'69–dc23

Manufactured in the United States of America

CPSIA Compliance Information: Batch #CWPK20. For Further Information contact Rosen Publishing, New York, New York at 1-800-237-9932.

CONTENTS

A DIFFERENT VIEW OF THE WORLD

Photographers show us places that the rest of us can't often see. They take pictures from the tops of mountains to the middle of oceans. How do photographers get to these places?

Not long ago, photographers risked their lives taking photos, or pictures, from the sky. They climbed mountains or flew in **helicopters** in bad weather. Military photographers traveled over enemy lands. Today, drones take most of these photos. Drones make it easier, and safer, for photographers to show us a new **perspective** of our world.

Drones make it possible to look into the mouth of an active volcano! The photographer is much safer too.

WHAT ARE DRONES?

Drones are also called unmanned **aerial vehicles** (UAVs). This means there's no onboard pilot, or person who flies the aircraft. Drones are flown by someone on the ground with a **remote control**. A computer can also tell drones where to fly.

The military uses drones to test explosives. Drones can also bring food and supplies to people during natural disasters—when bad weather ruins land and homes. They can even refuel another plane in the air! Drones are also used in sudden problems where a pilot may not be safe.

PARTS OF A DRONE (QUADCOPTER)

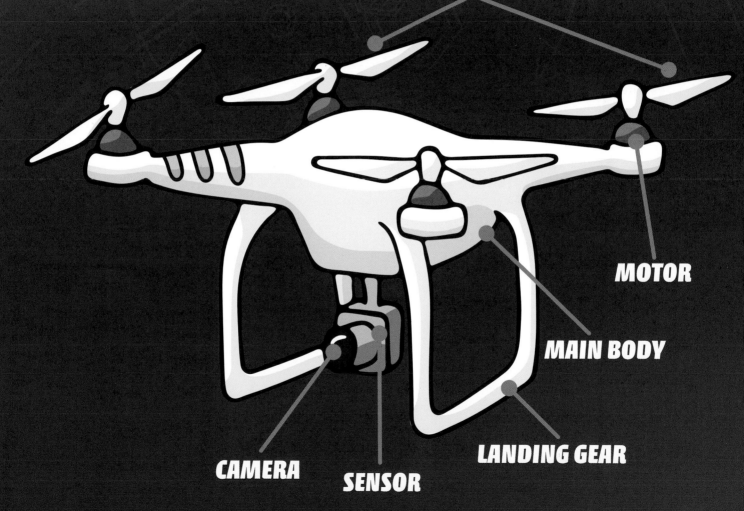

PROPELLERS

MOTOR

MAIN BODY

LANDING GEAR

CAMERA

SENSOR

PHOTOS IN THE SKY

Before drones, how did photographers take photos in the sky? In the 1880s, photographers attached cameras to hot air balloons, kites, and even rockets! When planes were invented in 1903, they were able to capture views that no one had ever seen before.

The first photo from space was taken on October 24, 1946 by a rocket sent to space from New Mexico. This led to the invention of **satellite** photography. Now, there are thousands of satellites circling Earth.

DRONE DETAILS

THE X-37B IS A SUPERSECRET SPACE DRONE. IT'S BEEN ON SEVERAL JOBS FOR THE AIR FORCE, CIRCLING EARTH FOR MONTHS. NO ONE BUT THE MILITARY KNOWS EVERYTHING IT DOES.

Satellites are drones in space. A weather satellite took this photo of a huge hurricane, or powerful storm with strong winds, near the Gulf of Mexico.

HISTORY OF THE DRONE

The first modern drones appeared in the 1980s. They were mostly used by the military when flying over enemy lands. Pilots no longer had to put their lives in danger.

In the late 1990s and early 2000s, drones became smaller, cheaper, and available to everyone. People started flying drones as a hobby. But photographers saw drones as something else. They saw a way to take photos from a point of view that people hadn't seen before—without ever having to leave the ground!

DRONE DETAILS

DRONES ARE SO POPULAR NOW THAT COMPANIES ARE INVENTING NEW WAYS TO USE THEM. SOME ARE MAKING DRONES THAT ARE SAFE TO USE INDOORS. ONE CHINESE COMPANY IS MAKING DRONES INTO TAXIS!

Quadcopters are one of the most popular kinds of hobby drones. They're called quadcopters because they have four propellers, or parts with blades that spin quickly to make the drone move.

WHY USE A DRONE?

Today's drones have cameras with **technology** that makes pictures come to life. The cameras **rotate** and can take pictures from every side. **Gyroscopes** keep the drone and camera steady so the pictures are clear.

Drones can be made to fly for miles and return home. Some can even avoid crashes! Photographers don't have to hike up mountains or through jungles anymore. They can get to the middle of a forest without moving an inch (2.5 cm).

DRONE DETAILS

TO AVOID ISSUES WHEN FLYING YOUR DRONE, IT'S IMPORTANT TO MAKE SURE THE BATTERIES, OR INSTRUMENTS THAT SUPPLY IT WITH ELECTRICITY, ARE PROPERLY CHARGED. MOST DRONE BATTERIES ONLY LAST FOR FLIGHTS UP TO ABOUT 30 MINUTES LONG.

Getting to an area like this could be a long and dangerous, or unsafe, trip. Drones make the job of a photographer much easier.

13

TURNING DRONES INTO ART

Everyday objects look completely different from 400 feet (122 m) above the ground. With drones, people can make simple pictures into something wonderful. Drones let photographers turn their photos into works of art.

Dirk Dallas is a drone photographer. He took regular photos for years and wanted to try something new. Now he takes all his photos with a drone. He controls the drone with a tablet so he can see what the camera sees. His photos show us the world in a new way.

DRONE DETAILS

CAMERA DRONES HAVE BECOME POPULAR AT WEDDINGS AND OUTSIDE PARTIES. PEOPLE PAY HUNDREDS, SOMETIMES THOUSANDS, OF DOLLARS TO SEE THEIR EVENTS FROM THE AIR.

A drone took this photo in Karaburun, Turkey, which wouldn't look as interesting from eye-level. Drones can show us new ways to look at ordinary things.

15

REACHING PEOPLE IN NEED

Drones are one of the best ways to get help to people during natural disasters. They can take pictures when crews can't reach the area. They can show us how much damage, or harm, was done and where people need to be saved.

Photojournalists, or news photographers, use drones to take photos and videos of disaster areas from safe places. This means they no longer have to travel into the middle of war zones, for example, to report the news.

DRONE DETAILS

THE **HUMANITARIAN** UAV NETWORK SHARES HOW DRONES HELP PEOPLE ALL OVER THE WORLD. THEY TEACH LOCAL COMMUNITIES THAT MIGHT BE HIT BY NATURAL DISASTERS HOW TO USE DRONES TO GET HELP.

Drones can get to a disaster scene faster than a manned plane. Their cameras show clear images in real time.

17

SURPRISING ACTION SHOTS

Before drones, sports photographers had to get creative. They would fly over stadiums in helicopters to get pictures of players. Drones now make overhead photos of your favorite sports easy to see. One drone can show us many different views at once. They're able to catch action photos at very fast speeds.

Coaches, the people who train athletes, can't see everything from the ground, so some use drones to take pictures of their team during games. Afterward, they study the pictures and use them to create winning plays.

Drone sports photography was first widely used in the 2014 Winter Olympics in Sochi, Russia. Now drones are used in sports photography all the time.

19

RULES OF THE SKY

There are rules for everyone who flies drones, even for fun. Drone pilots are accountable for knowing the rules and where it's OK to fly. As of 2019, drones should never fly above 400 feet (122 m). They're also not allowed near other aircraft or certain buildings. You can't fly a drone over large groups of people and you should avoid private property.

Photographers who take drone photos as a **career** are trained in how and where to fly. They have to pass a test before they can begin snapping pictures.

DRONE DETAILS

FLYING DRONES NEAR AIRPORTS, WILDFIRES, OR EMERGENCY AREAS WITHOUT PERMISSION IS AGAINST THE LAW. IT'S ALSO UNSAFE! DRONES CAN GET IN THE WAY OF OTHER AIRCRAFT, CAUSING ACCIDENTS.

Anyone can use a drone to take unbelievable pictures from the sky. But you must follow the rules!

DRONE PHOTOGRAPHY FOR FUN!

Drones are fun on their own. But drone photography can be a lively and interesting hobby. While your friends are taking pictures with their phones, you could be taking photos from more than 100 feet (60 m) above your house!

You don't have to be an expert, or master, to take beautiful aerial photos. Camera drones are cheaper and easier to use than ever. You just need to know the rules, such as where it's OK to fly. Then drones can take your photos to new heights!

GLOSSARY

aerial vehicle: Something used to transport people or things through the air.

career: A job a person can do for a long time.

gyroscope: A wheel mounted to spin rapidly and turn freely.

helicopter: An aircraft that flies using metal blades that turn around its top.

humanitarian: Having to do with a person or people who want to help others.

perspective: The way you see something; point of view.

photographer: Someone who takes pictures especially for a job or career.

remote control: A small machine used to control other electronic devices from a distance.

rotate: To turn around a center.

satellite: A man-made object that circles Earth, the moon, or another planet.

technology: A method that uses science to solve problems and the tools used to solve those problems.

INDEX

WEBSITES

Due to the changing nature of Internet links, PowerKids Press has developed an online list of websites related to the subject of this book. This site is updated regularly. Please use this link to access the list: www.powerkidslinks.com/dae/photog